Homes that Move

Raintree is an imprint of Capstone Global Library Limited, a company incorporated in England and Wales having its registered office at 7 Pilgrim Street, London, EC4V 6LB – Registered company number: 6695582

To contact Raintree:
Phone: 0845 6044371
Fax: + 44 (0) 1865 312263
Email: myorders@raintreepublishers.co.uk
Outside the UK please telephone +44 1865 312262.

Text © Capstone Global Library Limited 2014
First published in hardback in 2014
The moral rights of the proprietor have been asserted.

Edited by Daniel Nunn and Abby Colich
Designed by Cynthia Akiyoshi
Picture research by Mica Brancic
Production by Sophia Argyris
Originated by Capstone Global Library
Printed and bound in China at RR Donnelly Asia Printing Solutions

ISBN 978-1-4062-6323-7
17 16 15 14 13
10 9 8 7 6 5 4 3 2 1

British Library Cataloguing in Publication Data
Smith, Sian.
  Homes that move. -- (Where we live)
  1. Nomads--Dwellings--Juvenile literature. 2. Mobile homes--Juvenile literature.
  I. Title II. Series
  643.2-dc23.

Acknowledgements
We would like to thank the following for permission to reproduce photographs: Getty Images pp. 5 (Lonely Planet Images/Jane Sweeney); 7 (Image Source); 8 (Robert Harding World Imagery/C Gascoigne); 9 (AFP Photo/Anne-Christine Poujoulat); 10 (The Image Bank/Alan Powdrill); 14 (Lonely Planet Images/Scott Darsney); 15 (hemis.fr/Christophe Boisvieux); 17, 23 top (Panoramic Images); 18, centre top (Peter Arnold/Fred Bruemmer); 21 (Lonely Planet Images/Doug McKinlay); Library of Congress pp. 12, 23 centre bottom (Prints & Photographs Online Catalog); Shutterstock pp. 4, 22 bottom right (© Alexandra Lande); 6 (© Galyna Andrushko); 11 (© Baloncici); 16, 22 bottom left (© Tracing Tea); SuperStock pp. 13 (National Geographic); 19, 22 top left (age fotostock/Ton Koene); 20, 22 top right, 23 bottom (The Irish Image Collection).

Front cover photograph of a houseboat in Kerala, India, reproduced with permission of Shutterstock (© Alexandra Lande). Back cover photograph of nomads in the Kyrgyz Republic reproduced with permission of Shutterstock (© Tracing Tea).

Every effort has been made to contact copyright holders of material reproduced in this book. Any omissions will be rectified in subsequent printings if notice is given to the publisher.

Contents

Why do some homes move?

Some people live in homes
that move.

Some people keep moving so their animals can find food.

Some people keep moving to sell things in different places.

Some people keep moving to see new places.

Types of moving home

Some people live on houseboats.

Inside a houseboat there is a
bedroom and bathroom. There is
also a kitchen.

caravan

Some people live in homes on wheels.

Inside a mobile home, everything fits in a small space.

In the past, many people lived
in tents.

Tents are easy to put up and
take down.

Tents today

Some people live in tents today.

chum

Some people live in tents called chums. They move to find food for their reindeer.

yurt

Some people live in tents called yurts. Yurts can be made of wood and wool.

Bedouin tent

Some people live in tents in the desert. Tents in the desert give cover from the sun and wind.

Changing homes

igloo

blocks of snow

Sometimes people build a new home each time they move.

Some people live in igloos in the winter, and tents in the summer.

Moving together

Sometimes groups of people travel together.

Travelling as a group can help
people stay happy and safe.

Around the world

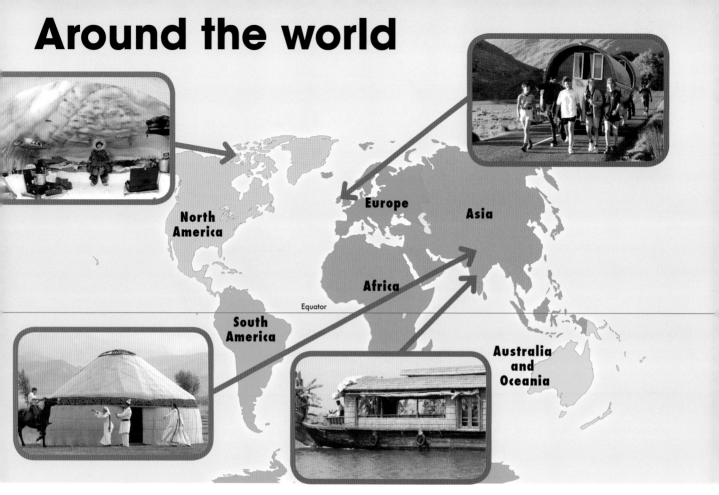

Follow the arrows to find out where each of these homes are.

More information on page 24

Picture glossary

 **desert** place that does not get much rain

 **igloo** home made from blocks of snow

 **tent** home made from poles covered with material

 **travel** to move around and see new places

23

Index

Photograph information

The photographs in this book were taken at the following locations: p. 4 Kerala, India; p. 5 Turmi, Africa; p. 6 Daraw, Egypt; p. 7 United States; p. 8 Kashmir, India; p. 9 Marseille, France; p. 10 Florida, United States; p. 12 United States; p. 13 Russia; p. 14 Omnogov, Asia; p. 15 Khovsgol Province, Mongolia (chum is pronounced "choom"); p. 16 Kyrgyz Republic; p. 17 Tunisia; p. 18 Canada; p. 19 Gojahaven, Canada; p. 20 County Mayo, Ireland; p. 21 Bamiyan, Afghanistan.

Notes for parents and teachers

Look at the title of the book and brainstorm types of moving home the children expect to find inside. Read the book together and discuss why people might need homes that can move. Compare the insides of different homes, for example the yurt (called a "ger" in Mongolia) on page 14 and the igloo on page 19. What do the two homes have in common? Discuss how homes provide us with a place to eat and sleep, and keep people and their things safe from the weather. Use the photograph information above to select a group of people to find out more about. Help the children to research the group and discuss the importance of community, traditions, and the feelings of belonging to part of a group.